DAHOMEY

The True Story Behind The movie The woman King

VIVIAN CHIBUIFE

All rights reserved. No part of this publication may be reproduced, distributed, or transmitted in any form or by any means, including photocopying, recording, or other electronic or mechanical methods, without the prior written permission of the publisher, except in the case of brief quotations embodied in critical reviews and certain other noncommercial uses permitted by copyright law.

Copyright © **Vivian Chibuife 2022**

TABLE OF CONTENT

INTRODUCTION

CHAPTER 1: BEFORE THE KINGDOM OF DAHOMEY
- Rise and expansion of the Empire (1600-1740)
- A localized power (1740-1852)
- Abolishing the slave trade (1852-1880)
- European settlement (1880-1900)

CHAPTER 2: THE STORY OF THE FEARLESS AMAZON WARRIORS OF DAHOMEY
- Amazon of Dahomey in 1890
- Political Position
- Battle and organization
- Disputes with nearby kingdoms

CHAPTER 3: THE SPARTAN WARS

- First Franco-Dahomean War
- War's root cause
- Battle of Cotonou
- The Atchoukpa Battle
- End of The War
- Second Franco-Dahomean War
- Escalation of Hostilities
- The Dogba War
- The Poguessa Battle
- Combat at Adégon
- Battle at Akpa
- End of Dahomey
- Conflict at Cana
- End Of The War
- Present Day Benin

INTRODUCTION

The history of the Kingdom of Dahomey, which is now Benin, is both lengthy and intricate. Its rulers and princes made choices that had a significant effect on the people who lived in the once-prosperous country.

Between around 1600 and 1904, the Kingdom of Dahomey saw a 300-year rise to dominance on the Atlantic coast of what is now Benin, becoming a significant force until the French occupation.

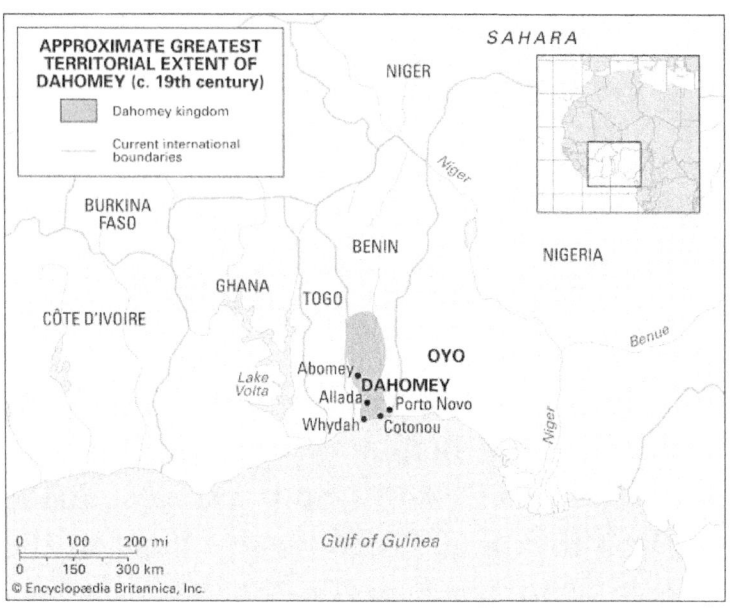

Map of Dahomey located in West Africa 1
Source Britannica

The kingdom of Dahomey (formerly known as Abomey) was established in western Africa on the Abomey plain by a fusion of many regional ethnic groupings.

The tribal clans, who may have been compelled to relocate because of the slave trade, came together under a highly organized, rigid military culture that was intended to protect and ultimately extend the tiny kingdom's frontiers.

When it overthrew the coastal kingdoms of Allada and Whydah in the 1720s, the kingdom rose to become a significant regional force. Up until 1852, when the British placed a naval blockade to end the trade, Dahomey was a significant hub for the Atlantic Slave Trade thanks to its control over these important coastal towns.

In 1892, hostilities with the French broke out, and in 1894, they seized control of the Kingdom of Dahomey. The French abdicated the kingdom in 1900, but the royal families and important government posts continued to have a significant influence on the politics of both the French government and the Republic of Dahomey after independence, which was renamed Benin in 1975. The kingdom's history has had a great influence on works that go much beyond those about African history, and it serves as the setting for many dramas and novels like Dora Milaje of Black Panther, the Dahomey warriors, and the festival movie The Woman King.

CHAPTER 1: BEFORE THE KINGDOM OF DAHOMEY

Evidence reveals that several minor tribes, known as the Gedevi, colonized the Abomey plateau before the kingdom of Dahomey was centralized.

The plateau, however, was very underdeveloped in comparison to the neighborhood due to a lack of resources and access to the main commercial routes in the area. The Oyo Empire (in modern-day Nigeria) was at the height of its strength and exerted some influence over the local tribes to the east of the Abomey plateau.

Two significant kingdoms with influence along the Atlantic coast, Allada and the Whydah, could be found to the south. Despite Portuguese engagement with the coastal region dating back to the 15th century, serious commerce did not begin until Grand-Popo and the Portuguese signed a trading pact in 1533.

The establishment of the Kingdom of Dahomey is the subject of several distinct folktales. Many of these tales, according to the majority of researchers, may only be loosely based on genuine occurrences since they were invented or greatly inflated in the 18th century to support the legitimacy of the Dahomey royal governments of the time.

The most prevalent creation story attributes the formation of the kingdom to Allada's royal ancestry. Following this legend, a Fon prince by the name of Agassu lived in Tado and attempted to become king. However, he was defeated and ended up ruling Allada instead. Two (or, in some tales, three) princes descended from Agassu battled over who would govern Allada in the year 1600.

It was determined that both princes would leave the town and establish separate kingdoms, with Do-Aklin migrating to the Abomey plateau in the north and Teagbanlin traveling south to start the city that would become Porto-Novo (Porto-Novo and the Kingdom of Dahomey remained rivals for much of history).

The Gedevi rulers in Abomey let Do-son Aklin's Dakodonu move there. The connection deteriorated, however, when Dakodonu asked a powerful chief called Dan for more territory.

With mockery, the chief asked Dakodonu, "Should I open up my belly and construct you a dwelling in it?" Dan was immediately murdered by Dakodonu, who also gave the order to erect his new palace there. The kingdom got its name from this event.

Rise and expansion of the Empire (1600-1740)

The Fon people

The Fon people, who had just arrived in the region, founded the empire in 1600. (or were possibly a result of intermarriage between the Aja people and the Gedevi). The Abomey Palace was built in the first half of the 17th century. Houegbadja (c. 1645–1685) is often regarded as the first monarch of the Kingdom of Dahomey. He constructed the Royal Palaces of Abomey and started plundering and occupying villages beyond the Abomey plateau.

The Kingdom of Whydah and Allada, as well as commerce with the Portuguese, Dutch, and British, all contributed to the growth of the slave trade in the coastal area at the same time. During this period, the Dahomey Kingdom started to be recognized by European merchants as a significant supplier of slaves for the Allada and Whydah slave markets.

When Houegbadja's grandson King Agaja assumed the throne in 1718, the Kingdom of Dahomey saw a remarkable period of growth. By 1720, King Agaja had renounced the kingdom's oath of fealty to Allada and had started stepping up military operations in the area. Agaja volunteered his army's assistance in 1724 to settle a succession dispute inside Allada.

He shifted his capital from Abomey to Allada by directing his soldiers against the Allada army and capturing the city. Agaja acquired control of Whydah in 1727, making them the dominant power along a wide portion of the coast. Agaja launched a series of cross-border incursions against the Oyo Empire in 1729 to start a war. The restoration of Whydah's royal dynasty to the throne during the battle made Agaja strive to retake the city. He moved a large chunk of his army, including a sizable percentage of female fighters at the rear (this is possibly the beginning of the Dahomey Amazons).

Because of their presumption that the Dahomey army had been depleted after the conflict with Oyo, the Whydah royal family evacuated the city upon witnessing such a sizable force. After the conflict with Oyo was over in 1730, Dahomey maintained internal sovereignty but joined the Oyo empire as a subject. By the conclusion of Agaja's rule, the Kingdom of Dahomey controlled a significant region, especially the key coastal towns involved in the slave traffic. At the same time, Agaja established the Annual Customs' important ceremony, known in Fon as Xwetanu, and most of the kingdom's administrative infrastructure.

A localized power (1740-1852)

After Agaja died in 1740, the empire was characterized by intense political conflict (albeit it was mainly contained behind the palace walls) and growing involvement in the slave trade. After Agaja's passing, there was a serious succession battle since Tegbessou was chosen instead of the legitimate successor (who ruled from 1740-1774). Tegbessou relocated the capital to Abomey but had to contend with several rival groups among the influential members of the kingdom and maintain the allegiance of acquired provinces. The empire also continued to conduct slave raids across the area and became a significant supplier to the Atlantic slave trade during this period. Dahomey responded by reducing some of its involvement in the slave trade in response to pressure from Oyo in the late 18th century, which was primarily intended to safeguard its slave trade. Even Nevertheless, the empire contributed significantly to the slave trade, making up to 20% of the total and giving the monarch the bulk of the trade's profits.

By violently removing his elder brother Adandozan from the throne in 1818, King Ghezo (reign 1818–1858) usurped the kingdom. The financial and military support of Francisco Félix de Sousa, a well-known Brazilian slave dealer based in Whydah, was crucial to Ghezo's ascent to power. De Sousa received far greater authority and wealth when Ghezo appointed him Whydah's viceroy of commerce, or chacha (the title chacha remains an important honorary position in Whydah to this day). Ghezo led soldiers against Oyo in 1823, ending Dahomey's position as a tributary and permanently weakening Oyo in the process.

<u>Abolishing the slave trade (1852-1880)</u>

The 1840s and 1850s saw two big shifts that profoundly affected Dahomey's politics. First, in the 1830s, the British, who had previously been a major buyer of slaves, started actively working to put an end to the slave trade. They dispatched many diplomatic delegations to Ghezo to persuade him to stop Dahomey's involvement in the trade, but all of them were rejected because Ghezo was afraid of the political repercussions of doing so. Second, after its founding in 1825, the city of Abeokuta gained notoriety as a refuge for individuals fleeing Dahomey's slave raids.

Dahomey and Abeokuta fought a war in 1844, and Abeokuta won. The conflict between Abeokuta and Dahomey for economic dominance in the area was further solidified by more bloodshed in the early 1850s.

The pressure caused a variety of adjustments within. While Ghezo resisted British demands to halt the slave trade, the trade in palm oil as a substitute for slavery started to grow considerably at the same time. Politically, the Elephant and the Fly political parties started to dominate the discussion.

The Elephant promoted the continuation of the slave trade and resistance to British pressure via its connections to Ghezo, prominent political figures, and the creole slave dealers like the family of De Sousa. In contrast, the Fly group sought accommodation with Abeokuta and the British to increase the trade in palm oil. This party was made up of several chiefs and a loose coalition of palm oil growers.

These two groups engaged in a series of contentious disputes over the future of the Kingdom of Dahomey during the policy and war deliberations conducted at the Annual Customs.

To pressure Dahomey to stop the slave trade, the British put a naval blockade on its ports in the years 1851–1852. Ghezo ratified a pact with the British in January 1852 that put a halt to the export of slaves from Dahomey.

Ghezo put a stop to extensive military operations and human sacrifice in the kingdom that year and the year after. Political pressure nonetheless had a role in the revival of the slave trade and extensive military operations in 1857 and 1858. After Ghezo was killed by an Abeokuta-affiliated sniper, the two nations' large-scale hostilities started in 1864.

This one again went in Abeokuta's favor, and as a consequence, the slave trade was unable to be fully restored to its 1850 level. Slave merchants' influence in the empire waned as the palm oil trade grew in importance as a sector of the economy.

European settlement (1880-1900)

Dahomey's continuous dominance over important coastal towns made the region a critical position in the European race for Africa. Although taxation of the King of Dahomey was to continue, the Kingdom of Dahomey consented in 1878 for the French to turn the city of Cotonou into a protectorate. Similar concessions were made to the French in 1883 about Porto-Novo, a longtime coastal competitor of Dahomey.

Following the death of King Glele in 1889, his son Béhanzin assumed the throne and turned discussions with the French somewhat hostile. The pact with France that granted them Cotonou was abandoned by Béhanzin, who then started plundering the property. When Béhanzin started conducting slave raids on French protectorates along the coast, particularly Grand-Popo, in 1891, tensions reached a peak. The French military concluded in that year that a military takeover was the only option, and General Alfred-Amédée Dodds was given command of the operation, which was set to begin in 1892.

From January 1892 to January 1894, the Franco-Dahomean War lasted. On January 15, 1894, Dodds took the city of Abomey and King Béhanzin (January 25). The defeat of the Dahomey Amazons in November 1892 was notable during the conflict. Agoli-agbo was installed as the new king of Dahomey by Dodds, who banished Béhanzin to French colonies in the Caribbean in part because he was seen to be the most pliable of the possibilities. The French started making significant changes to the Kingdom of Dahomey's politics and administration. Agoli-Agbo opposed the French's introduction of a new poll tax in 1899, which led to significant political issues in the protectorate. Agoli-Agbo was overthrown by the French on February 17, 1900, putting an end to the Kingdom of Dahomey. However, as the leaders of cantons, the French gathered several important kingdom officials. The Kingdom of Dahomey, Porto-Novo, and a region to the north under loose tribal rule were all included in French Dahomey.

Because of his crucial role in Fon ancestor worship and rituals, Agoli-Agbo was banished from 1900 to 1910, when the French authority decided to let him return to the region. The French authority permitted him to visit Abomey to take part in ceremonial duties at the Annual Customs, but he was not permitted to live there or travel at will.

Political history

From 1900 until 1960, when Dahomey obtained independence and adopted the name Republic of Dahomey, the region was still under French rule. Benin replaced the Republic of Dahomey as the nation's name in 1975. Both under French rule and after independence, the King of Dahomey had a significant ceremonial role. Since 2000, there has been conflict over the throne between Agoli-Agbo III and Houedogni Behanzin, who both have competing claims.

Following independence, Dahomey and Benin continued to rely on the political and economic hierarchy of Dahomey. Justin Ahomadégbé-Tomêtin, who served as the nation's head of state twice, was a crucial figure in the triumvirate that ruled politics in the nation from 1960 to 1972. Justin attained substantial political clout thanks to his ties to the Dahomey royal family. The descendants of Francisco Félix de Sousa continue to play crucial roles in Benin's politics today. Examples include Colonel Paul-Émile de Souza, who served as the nation's leader from 1969 to 1970, and Isidore de Souza, who served as the country's national assembly president from 1990 to 1991.

Kojo Tovalou Houénou (1887–1936), a prominent opponent of the French colonial empire who claimed to be a prince of Dahomey but spent the majority of his life there, founded the Ligue Universelle pour la Défense de la Race Noire to fight for the inclusion of Africans as full citizens of the French state.

The origin of mankind and the cradle of civilization are now recognized as being on the African continent.

CHAPTER 2: THE STORY OF THE FEARLESS AMAZON WARRIORS OF DAHOMEY

Amazon warriors of Dahomey

Without acknowledging the women who strengthened the Kingdom of Dahomey's military might, no account of the country is complete.

There was a powerful army of all-female warriors in Dahomey, in the modern-day Republic of Benin, from the 18th until the late 19th century. Due to their resemblance to the Amazons from Greek mythology, they were also referred to as the Mino (our Mothers) or Ahosi (kings' wives) by European observers.

It's not quite known where the Amazons came from. It was credited to King Houegbadja, the third King of Dahomey, who reigned from 1645 until 1685. According to legend, Houegbadja began the organization that would become the Amazons as a group of elephant hunters known as the Gbeto.

Another story said that Queen Hangbe, who ruled from 1708 to 1711, organized a squad of female royal bodyguards. She was Houegbadja's daughter. Tradition has it that her brother, King Agaja, who succeeded her, used them to help Dahomey overcome the neighboring kingdom of Savi in 1727.

The Amazons did, however, only start to play a significant role in the Dahomean military during the reign of King Ghezo (reigning from 1818 to 1858). Ghezo was renowned for reforming the military. He gave the army priority, boosting its funding and formalizing its organization to become a genuine force.

Several thousand women were said to have served as soldiers for Dahomey in the middle of the nineteenth century, making up about 30–40% of the army.

Ghezo enlisted male and female troops from foreign prisoners. Although free Dahomean women were also used to recruit women soldiers, some of them enlisted as early as 8 years old. In Fon culture, some women enlisted as warriors on their initiative, while others were forced to do so after their husbands or fathers complained to the monarch about their behavior.

Being a member of the Mino was intended to refine any aggressive personality qualities for the sake of battle. They were not permitted to marry or have children while they were members (though they were legally married to the king). They included many virgins.

Amazon of Dahomey in 1890

The Mino engaged in rigorous physical training. Through military training that included assaulting acacia-thorn defenses and beheading captives, they learned survival skills and indifference to suffering and death. The focus was on discipline.

When Jean Bayol, a French naval commander, visited Abomey in December 1889, he saw a test being administered to Nanisca, a young recruit "who had not yet murdered anybody." She was brought before a juvenile prisoner who was imprisoned and sitting in a basket.

"walked briskly up to, swinging her sword three times with both hands, then cutting the rest of the flesh connecting the head to the trunk with calm precision... She then drank the blood she had squeezed off her weapon.

Seh-Dong-Hong-Beh, a leader of the Dahomey Amazon warriors – drawn by Frederick Forbes in 1851

The Mino provided women with the chance to "advance to positions of authority and influence" in a setting designed for personal empowerment.

The Mino was a powerful and affluent people. According to the renowned traveler Sir Richard Burton, who visited Dahomey in the 1860s, Gezo's female army resided in his courtyard and was kept well-supplied with tobacco, whiskey, and slaves—as many as 50 to each fighter.

The slave girl holding the bell led the way for the amazons as they left the castle. Every guy was instructed by the sound to move out of their way, retreat a particular distance, and turn away.

The right and left wings, as well as the elite center wing or Fanti, made up the three primary wings of the women's army.

These wings were divided into five subgroups: Gulohento (Riflewomen) were effective fighters in close quarters and each carried a long rifle and a short sword. Gbeto (Huntresses) were formerly a corps of elephant huntresses. Some of them carried spears and small swords, including Nyekplohento (Reapers), who were few but very feared. They had very sharp blades that could sever a man in half with a single strike, and the Gohento (Archers) were masters at using bows and arrows. The best young females were chosen to be the Agbalya (Gunners), who used the army's artillery, including ancient iron cannons from the seventeenth century and German Krupp cannons that Europeans had given to the Kingdom of Dahomey. Their hooked and poisoned arrows almost ever missed their targets.

The amazon women played a significant role in the conflicts with nearby countries, often seizing prisoners for the slave trade.

However, they lost quite a few battles. Notable was the unsuccessful attempts to invade Abeokuta, the Egbas' capital, in 1851 and 1864. the first and second Franco-Dahomean Wars, as well. When the

French overran Dahomey in 1892, they were especially brutal against the Amazons, killing many of them in part because they realized that the female warriors had been the final line of defense against their invasion.

Even their adversaries praised the daring Dahomeyan female warriors for their bravery. They were praised as "warrioresses... battle with tremendous heroism, constantly ahead of the other soldiers," according to Bern, a member of the French Foreign Legion. They are very fearless, combat-trained, and disciplined.

Political Position

The Mino played a significant part in the Grand Council's discussion on the kingdom's policies. They favored the trade in palm oil above the traffic in slaves from the 1840s to the 1870s (when the opposition party disintegrated), during which time they typically backed peace with Abeokuta and improved economic ties with England. They disagreed with their male military colleagues as a result of this.

In addition to the council, the Annual Customs of Dahomey included a parade, a review of the military, and an oath-taking by the soldiers in front of the monarch. A pretend battle in which Amazons stormed a "fort" and "captured" the slaves within was part of the festivities on the 27th day of the Annual Customs, as the priest Francesco Borghero noted in his journals.

Battle and organization

The female troops underwent rigorous training and received uniforms. According to estimates made by travelers, by the middle of the 19th century, they numbered between 1,000 and 6,000 women, or almost a third of the total Dahomey army. These verified sources also said that the female troops endured several setbacks.

The king's bodyguards were supposed to form the core of the women soldiers' organizational system, which was parallel to that of the whole army. Each flank was commanded by a different commander. According to certain tales, every male soldier had a female warrior partner.

According to one English observer's report from the middle of the 19th century, ladies who had three stripes of whitewash around each leg were given distinguishing marks.

The Dahomean women warriors of the later era carried Winchester rifles, clubs, and knives. Units were commanded by women. According to a translation of a women's battle song that was published in 1851, the warriors would chant,

"The same way a blacksmith takes an iron bar and modifies it by fire, we have altered our nature. We are now men, no longer women."

This demonstrates the idea that a woman who fights becomes a man and that fighters cannot be women.

Disputes with nearby kingdoms

The Dahomey kingdom required prisoners for the slave trade because it often fought its neighbors. The Barracoon nonfiction book by Zora Neale Hurston makes mention of the Dahomey women warriors who participated in slave raids and the futile campaigns against Abeokuta.

Dissolution and legacy
When France took over as the kingdom's protector, the soldiers were dissolved.
According to oral history, several of the remaining amazons hid in Abomey later and killed many French officers there. Other accounts claim that the ladies offered to

defend Agoli-Agbo, the brother of Béhanzin, and disguised themselves as his wife to do so.

While some of the ladies got married and had kids, others stayed single. The lives of over two dozen ex-amazons were studied by a historian, who found that all the women had trouble transitioning to life after being warriors and often struggled to find new positions in their communities that gave them a feeling of pride equivalent to their old existence. Many had a propensity to initiate disagreements or conflicts that alarmed their neighbors and loved ones.

Between 1934 and 1942, several British tourists in Abomey documented their interactions with former amazons who were now elderly ladies who either spun cotton or lazed in courtyards.

After the Dahomey Amazons were dissolved, it is said that an undetermined number of women continued the tradition by training alongside the group's members. They were never in a battle.

CHAPTER 3: THE SPARTAN WARS

First Franco-Dahomean War

First Franco-Dahomean War l Source Alamy

Under the command of General Alfred-Amédée Dodds, France engaged in battle with Dahomey, whose ruler was King Béhanzin, in the First Franco-Dahomean War, which broke out in 1890. The Battle of Abomey ended in victory for the French.

During the second part of the 19th century, European advance into West Africa accelerated, and in 1890 King Béhanzin began engaging French soldiers during the First Franco-Dahomean War. The ladies "handled brilliantly" in hand-to-hand fighting, according to European witnesses, although they shot their flintlocks from the hip rather than the shoulder.

European nations were busily occupying and colonizing most of Africa by the end of the 19th century. The French Third Republic was the primary colonial authority in what is now Benin. The Fon kingdom of Dahomey, one of the most powerful powers in West Africa at the time, was one of the indigenous peoples with whom the French had established trade links.

A Franco-Dahomean friendship pact that permitted French business operations and missionaries to enter the nation was ratified in 1851.

The Fon kingdom of Dahomey was at its pinnacle of dominance by 1890. It claimed almost the whole present Benin coast as well as a sizable portion of south-central Benin up to Atcheribé. The little kingdom of Porto-Novo, which was close to the shore, was one of Dahomey's most significant tributaries. Since the middle of the 18th century, there has been intermittent conflict between the kingdom and Dahomey.

British anti-slavery ships stormed Porto-Novo in 1861. In 1863, Porto-Novo requested and obtained French protection, but Dahomey refused it.

The status of Cotonou, a port the French claimed was within their jurisdiction due to a treaty signed by a delegate of Dahomey in Whydah, was another point of disagreement. Dahomey continued to levy duties at the port while disobeying any French claims there as well.

War's root cause

After Dahomey invaded the kingdom in 1882, King Toffa I reinstituted French protection in Porto-Novo in 1874.

Dahomey proceeded to invade the town, which resulted in an event that sparked a conflict between the French and the Fon. Dahomey invaded Ouémé town in March 1889 when the chief was protected by the French. The Fon ordered one of his Dahomey Amazons to behead him and wrap his head in the flag after saying that it would shield him. France then sent a delegation to the capital of Dahomey, Abomey, in March of that year to make its claims to Cotonou known and propose an annual payment. The assignment was given to the crown prince, who ultimately became king Béhanzin, but little was accomplished but growing mistrust among them.

In response to these events, France increased its presence in Cotonou to 359 troops, of which 299 were Tirailleurs or Senegalese and Gabonese with French training.

In Cotonou, the French detained the top Fon authorities on February 21 and started reinforcing the area. Additionally, clashes with the local militia occurred.

It didn't take long for Abomey to hear about this. Cotonou was intended to be permanently returned to Fon authority, thus Dahomey despatched a force there right away.

Battle of Cotonou

The Amazons took part in just one significant battle, the Cotonou conflict, in which tens of thousands of Dahomey (many of them Amazons) attacked the French lines and battled the defenders in hand-to-hand combat. With the gunning down of many hundred Dahomey soldiers, the Amazons were soundly defeated. 129 Dahomey men reportedly died in melee fighting within the French lines.

On March 4, at about five in the morning, a Dahomey army of several thousand men stormed the wood stockade around Cotonou. This was typical of the Dahomeyan Fon army, which almost always marched at night and launched attacks soon before daybreak.

The Fon shot into the cage by tearing the posts apart and forcing their muskets through.

Some were able to scale the 800-meter boundary, causing casualties within the fortified walls. The Fon army retreated after four hours of fierce combat, most of which was conducted hand-to-hand against overwhelming French artillery and even gunboat shelling.

The Fon lost several hundred people, while the French suffered very few casualties (129 within the French lines).

The Atchoukpa Battle

During the First Franco-Dahomean War, on April 20, 1890, the Battle of Atchoukpa took place close to the town of Atchoukpa. A group of 7,000 Dahomey warriors and 2,000 Dahomey Amazons led by King Béhanzin were attempting to march on Porto-Novo when a French force of 350 soldiers under Colonel Terrillon and 500 of King Toffa I's men temporarily helped them.

The First Franco-Dahomean War's last significant battle was the Battle of Atchoukpa.

As a consequence of the Dahomey raids against the French protectorate of Porto-Novo, the French detained many Dahomey leaders in Cotonou on April 21, 1890, thus starting the First Franco-Dahomean War. A significant Dahomey assault on Cotonou was repelled on March 4 following a violent struggle.

King Béhanzin's troops crossed the Ouémé River on April 15, 1890. They marched toward Porto-Novo, burning numerous towns on their way, and ultimately pitched up camp a few kilometers north of the city.

Leaving Porto-Novo at 6 a.m. on April 20, a 350-man French column made up of companies of Senegalese Tirailleurs and Troupes de Marines headed for the Dahomey army. They traveled with 500 Porto-Novo warriors from the area.

A little after 7:30 in the morning, Dahomey and French soldiers battled in the squares. King Toffa I's soldiers, who were leading the French column, came under Dahomey fire in the hamlet of Atchoukpa.

They instantly went into disarray after the short fusillade, which left 8 of them dead and several more injured.

The leading French company, led by Captain Arnoux, set up shop to cover Toffa's troops' withdrawal as they fled in terror toward Porto-Novo.

Colonel Terrillon ordered his soldiers to form infantry squares as the Dahomey army emerged from the town and headed toward the French.

Béhanzin's force, which included 7,000 soldiers and 2,000 Dahomey Amazons, engaged French squares in repeated attacks for more than an hour without result.

Each of their attempts was repelled by superior French artillery and discipline, which also caused them to suffer horrendous fatalities.

King Béhanzin decided to dispatch a detachment to avoid them to burn down Porto-Novo while his main army kept the French engaged at approximately 9:00 a.m.

after seeing that his soldiers were failing to harm the French squares.

However, Colonel Terrillon saw the maneuver right away and ordered his squares to move in the direction of the detachment. The French opened fire on the Dahomey detachment as soon as they were in range, swiftly routing the Dahomey group.

The combat continued for another hour or so as French squares continued to slowly retreat toward Porto-Novo to prevent any more attempts to circumvent them.

Béhanzin ultimately gave the order to leave at about 10:00 a.m., abandoning his ambitions to assault Porto-Novo.

Result of the conflict

33 French soldiers were injured, including 1 commander, 15 white French soldiers, and

17 Senegalese tirailleurs. The soldiers of King Toffa I suffered 8 fatalities and 20 wounds in their short first encounter. Dahomey suffered far worse casualties, having lost more than 1,500 people to the war.

The First Franco-Dahomean War came to an end with the Battle of Atchoukpa, and King Béhanzin would not make any further efforts to take Porto-Novo. The French despatched small reconnaissance missions the next day, and they learned that Béhanzin's soldiers had completely evacuated from the area around the city and were no longer present beyond the Ouémé River.

End of The War

Cotonou and Porto-Novo were not subject to any more raids from Dahomey. Dahomey signed a contract on October 3, 1890, recognizing the kingdom of Porto-Novo as a protectorate of France. In exchange for giving up his customs rights, Béhanzin received 20,000 francs a year in addition to being obliged to relinquish Cotonou.

The war was a spectacular success for France while being humiliating yet enlightening for Dahomey. Despite the deal, both parties anticipated another decisive conflict since they thought the current state of calm could not survive. Despite the truce, hostilities rapidly resumed, intensifying into the Second Franco-Dahomean War two years later.

Second Franco-Dahomean War

Second Franco-Dahomean War | Source Alamy

Between 1892 and 1894, France and Dahomey were at war in the Second Franco-Dahomean War, which was fought under the command of General Alfred-Amédée Dodds. Coming out on top, the French added Dahomey to their expanding colonial holdings in French West Africa.

The First Franco-Dahomean War was fought in 1890 between the Fon kingdom of Dahomey and the French Third Republic over the former's claims to certain regions, particularly those in the Ouémé Valley. After two military setbacks at the hands of the French, the Fon ended hostilities, withdrew their men, and agreed to all of France's demands in a treaty.

Dahomey immediately re-armed with contemporary weaponry in preparation for a second, conclusive struggle, even though it remained a formidable power in the region.

The Fon resumed raiding the same valley that was fought over in the first battle with France after re-arming and reorganizing. The French Resident in Porto-Novo, Victor Ballot, was sent upriver on a gunboat to investigate. Five guys were wounded when his ship was assaulted and forced to leave the area.

King Béhanzin dismissed the French accusations, and the French quickly launched the war.

Alfred-Amédée Dodds, an octoroon colonel of the Troupes de marine from Senegal, was given responsibility by the French for the military effort against Dahomey. In addition to the dependable tirailleurs, Colonel Dodds brought 2,164 men with him, including Foreign Legionnaires, marines, engineers, artillery, and spahis, a kind of Senegalese cavalry.

These troops were equipped with brand-new Lebel weapons, which would be crucial in the next conflict. Additionally, the 2,600 porters from the Porto-Novo kingdom, a French protectorate, were brought to the battle.

The Fon had accumulated between 4,000 and 6,000 firearms, including Mannlicher and Winchester carbines, before the start of the second war. These were bought from German traders via the Whydah port. The usage of the machine guns and Krupp cannons that King Béhanzin also purchased is unknown (and improbable).

Escalation of Hostilities

To stop any more shipments of weapons, the French blockaded Dahomey's shore on June 15, 1892. The first shots of the war were then fired on July 4 by French gunboats when they shelled several towns in the lower Ouémé Valley. Midway through August, the meticulously planned French force started to advance inland in preparation for its eventual arrival in Abomey, the capital of Dahomey.

The Dogba War

On September 14, about 80 kilometers (50 miles) upriver at the boundary of Dahomey and Porto-Novo, the French invasion army gathered in the settlement of Dogba. On September 19, at approximately 5:00 a.m., a Dahomey army assaulted the French troops.

After three to four hours of nonstop battling, which included several Fon attempts at physical combat, the Fon finally stopped the assault. While the French army only lost five soldiers, hundreds of Fons were left dead on the battlefield.

The Poguessa Battle

Before reversing course and heading west in the direction of Abomey, the French soldiers advanced another 24 km (15 mi) upriver. On October 4, Fon soldiers led by King Béhanzin personally assaulted the French army at Poguessa (sometimes spelled Pokissa or Kpokissa).

Over two to three hours, the Fon launched several ferocious attacks, but they were all repulsed by the French 20-inch bayonets. 200 troops from the Dahomey army were lost before they were forced to retreat. With just 42 losses, the French won the battle. The Dahomey Amazons stood out throughout the conflict as well.

The Fon switched from set-piece confrontations to guerilla tactics after their loss at Poguessa. The 40 km (25 km) march by the French invading army from Poguessa to the last significant fight at Cana, just outside of Abomey, took them a month. To stop the French invasion, the Fon fought from trenches and foxholes.

Combat at Adégon

The French and Fon engaged in yet another significant battle on October 6 at the hamlet of Adégon. The Fon performed poorly once again, losing 417 Dahomey Amazons and 86 Dahomey regulars.

Six people were killed and 32 were injured in France. The majority of Dahomey's casualties were caused by the French bayonet attack. The royal court lost optimism after the fight, which marked a turning point for Dahomey. [10] The loss of a large portion of Dahomey's Amazon corps made the conflict noteworthy as well.

Battle at Akpa

After Adégon, the French column was able to go another 24 km (15 mi) in the direction of Abomey before bivouacking near the community of Akpa. They have been assaulted every day since they came.

Dahomey's Amazons were missing from the time the French arrived until 14 October. Some women were reportedly present on the front lines of the Dahomean army on October 15 when they were routed by a Legion unit following a bayonet assault. Before fire from the Legion section "demolished the entire rank" of the Dahomean infantry that the Amazon had commanded, the battalion commander was reportedly shot in the chest from close range by an Amazon. On October 26, after receiving fresh supplies, the French evacuated Akpa and moved toward Cotopa.

End of Dahomey

The French engaged the Dahomey soldiers at Cotopa and other locations from October 26 to 27 while navigating enemy trench lines. Nearly all conflicts were decided by bayonet charges. Dahomey's swords and machetes were readily outclassed by French bayonets due to the Fon tribe's preference for hand-to-hand combat. The French claim that the Amazons put up the most of a fight, rushing out of their trenches but to no effect.

Conflict at Cana

The French and Fon soldiers engaged in combat on the outskirts of Cana from November 2 to November 4. At this point, including slaves and released prisoners, Béhanzin's army totaled no more than 1,500 men. The monarch ordered the assault on the French bivouac on November 3. The majority of the troop seemed to be made up of amazons. The Fon army retreated after four hours of vain fighting. Up until the next morning, there was fighting.

Amazons were last used at the engagement at Cana, which took place in the settlement of Diokoué, which had a royal palace. Targeting French officers was given to specialized Amazonian forces. After a full day of combat, the French used a second bayonet charge to overtake the Dahomey force.

<u>End Of The War</u>

Dahomey dispatched the French on a ceasefire mission on November 5; the French entered Cana the next day. However, the peace mission was unsuccessful, and on November 16, the French troops invaded Abomey.

To prevent the city from falling into enemy hands, King Béhanzin set the city on fire and ordered its evacuation. On November 17, when the French invaded the city, he and the remaining Dahomey army units withdrew to the north. The Singboji palace, which survived the fire and is still standing in present-day Benin, was draped in the French tricolor.

Atcheribé, 48 km (30 km) north of the city, was the monarch of Dahomey when he escaped. The army's Amazon corps was attempted to be rebuilt before the French selected Goutchili, Béhanzin's brother, as the new king.

On January 15, 1894, King Béhanzin submitted to the French and was sent to Martinique. The conflict was formally over.

In 1894, the kingdom was diminished and turned into a protectorate of France. The region joined French Dahomey, a French colony, in 1904.

Present Day Benin

French Dahomey became the Republic of Dahomey, a self-governing colony, in 1958. It attained complete independence in 1960.

The People's Republic of Benin was given to it in 1975, and the Republic of Benin was given to it in 1991.

The kingdom is still in existence today as a Benin-based component monarchy. The constitution of Benin no longer grants its monarchs any formal authority, although they continue to have some political and economic sway. Important Vodun religious festivals and other customary rites are attended by contemporary rulers.

Printed in Great Britain
by Amazon